FAITH
like SKIN

**A JOURNEY OF LEARNING TO DISPLAY FAITH
THROUGH THE CHALLENGES OF CANCER,
DEATH, & BROKEN RELATIONSHIPS**

by Hannah Dekker Keels

kelley *creative*

Rowlett, TX USA

ISBNs:
978-1-7345677-2-4   Paperback
978-1-7345677-3-1   eBook

TABLE OF CONTENTS

This book is dedicated to my sons Liam, Lance, Logan, & Lucas, to my bestie in Heaven, Sara, and to my bestie on earth who doubles as my husband and Twinkie, Chuck. You all teach me to go to Jesus. Every moment of every day.

FOREWORD

I met Hannah in 1995 when I moved to New Jersey. Four years later she was a bridesmaid in my wedding, and from then on we shared life as sisters-in-law. Moves. Pregnancies. Babies. Before long there were seven boys between our two families. We shared the boy-mom bond and unique friendship that comes from being married to brothers. When we settled within an hour of each other in southeast Pennsylvania, our efforts to get our kids together forged fond memories: autumn corn mazes, Christmas gift exchanges, Easter egg hunts, and sleepovers. Every summer, in Hannah's kitchen, we'd make gallons of salsa with farm fresh ingredients. After a full afternoon, I'd drive home with at least a dozen mason jars clinking in the back of my minivan. I'll never forget the time we forgot to wear gloves while dicing jalapenos. Hannah's resourcefulness kicked in. We tried everything from lime juice to yogurt to stop the burn. We can laugh at it now!

My family and I missed Hannah and her family when they moved to Arizona in 2015. Those rhythms of togetherness changed. A few months after their move, we flew out to see "the cousins" in sunny Phoenix. Shortly after we returned to the snowy Northeast, we got a phone call. The events that followed are explained in this book.

If you meet Hannah, the first thing you notice is her natural beauty. As you get to know her, you find her radiance is more than skin deep. She is smart, strong, industrious, and adventurous. She is caring, wise, nurturing, and creative. She's an amazing cook! With an eye for detail, she creates beauty in all that extends from her—fashion, home, meals, art. Hannah was slightly ahead of me in marriage and motherhood, so I leaned on her for advice. Her open home and joy in serving others inspired me. Her faith was steady. As the events of this book unfold before you, you will see what I had the honor to witness in real-time: a soul transformed by suffering.

Hannah experienced a series of tragedies. Powerless, I watched her endure loss after breath-taking loss. Along with commiting to pray, I began to check-in via text every Friday. Eventually, those texts became more frequent, and visits followed. Although we no longer shared a family name, our friendship flourished. C.S. Lewis wrote, "Friendship is born at that moment when one person says to another: 'What! You too? I thought I was the only one!'" We discovered such moments, realizing we could talk with ease about the hard stuff of life, our mid-life journeys, and the spiritual renewal we were both experiencing. We found a shared vision: a Godward life of worship, prayer, and surrender to His will in everything.

I watched what could have made Hannah bitter and depressed become a chrysalis. Something sacred was happening. Weeping slowly gave way to joy; pain molded to purpose. "Beauty from ashes" was rising. Hope was born. Hannah's life proves our losses are not the end of our story. They are the doorway to more, if we surrender all to Jesus, lay down our defenses, and wear our faith like skin.

—*Linda Cerynik*

I: THE FIVE LOSSES

Do you know what the five most stressful events of life are? I googled them. Research shows they include moving, divorce, death of a loved one, job loss, and major illness. Any one of them is enough to significantly sideline a person. I had all five happen to me in the span of three-and-a-half years. So much loss. Some days I just rode the torrential waves of grief as I mired my way through the unending drama of paperwork, court dates, medical appointments, and financial strain. Some days the sharp shrapnel of sin and brokenness hit me harder than others and roughened the already raw edges of my grief. But I wasn't alone in any of it. God had a plan. Jesus reminded me that He wept. He knew what it was to experience the grief of loss.

Suffering. *Loss*. None of us are exempt from it. We all feel the tentacles now and then, reaching out to us, trying to entwine around us—to wrap us up and submerge us. Over the last four years of my life I became entirely too well acquainted with it. Loss has become a familiar, although unwelcome, space in my life. And as I realized how easy it is to go to despair and bitterness in my suffering, God reached in with His long arm of mercy and brought me His hope and His love. He breathed life into my soul, filled me with His incredible peace, and reminded me He calls me Child. He taught me that He is always good.

You are holding this book because God impressed on my heart to tell my faith story. My friend Elly texted me one day and said she had a dream that I was to "write a book and would be speaking in churches." I had no idea about the speaking in churches part, but through her, God sent the confirmation I needed. Now I was sure I had to write my story!

1 Chronicles 16:8-9,12 (NASB) says, "Oh give thank to the Lord, call upon His name; Make known His deeds among the peoples. Sing to Him, sing praises to Him; Speak of all His wonders. *Remember* His wonderful deeds which He has done…" This book is *my remembering*. One of my cousins referred to me as "a living miracle in motion." I want to record His works and tell His stories.

It was a stunning revelation to me that He could use my brokenness. He emptied me so completely of all of my "mis-worship"— all the stuff that I was allowing to fill up my life. I was not worshiping in Spirit and in Truth (John 4:24). And once He emptied me, He filled me up to overflowing so I could spill out onto those around me. It was so humbling to realize that I could be His vessel. I was awestruck that He chose me for this. The High King of Heaven, the God of *all* the universe loves and moves *through* us with His Spirit and uses *us*. He uses my "broken pot" to reach others in their hurts and sorrows.

We are like common clay jars that carry this glorious treasure within, so that the extraordinary overflow of power will be seen as God's, not ours 2 Corinthians 4:7.

Over and over, I found myself in situations I didn't like, dealing with things I never wanted, expected, or planned. I never imagined a life so full of loss could become a blessing.

This is an amazing story of how God transformed a broken and lonely girl into a joy-filled and radically transformed woman.

II: The Monster Within

I had noticed a lump in the side of my right breast several months before. Never having felt anything before, I figured it was a cyst. I told myself I would watch it for a month and see if it went away. I had never done regular self-exams. Something felt off. Feeling uneasy, I finally googled a local breast center and scheduled an appointment.

I had been invited by one of the eye surgeons I worked with to go on a medical mission trip to Fiji. I agreed to go since I could use my nursing skills to help perform cataract surgery, and enjoy Fiji. My breast ultrasound was scheduled for July 28 at 9:30 in the morning, the day before my trip. My doctor did not like the look of my lump and immediately called upstairs to make a mammography appointment and another higher-level ultrasound.

I was anti mammogram. I always err on the alternative side of treatment. This was not what I wanted. But I needed answers. So I reluctantly went upstairs and was ushered into a spa-like environment with plush robes, comfy couches, and water bottles—everything but the massage. I spent hours waiting to be fit into the schedule. After my first introduction to a mammogram and eventually a high definition ultrasound, the doctor that read my results came in and sat down with me. She was the first person to utter the word *cancer* to me. She held me in her arms and let me cry. And she offered the first words of encouragement to me, words I desperately needed to hear. "You can beat this, Hannah."

I made a follow-up appointment for a biopsy on August 11, the morning after I was to return from Fiji. They would take a sample of my tumor to see what I was dealing with. I was glad they didn't discourage me from going on my trip—for ten days I escaped reality. After the biopsy, I managed my way to my car and wept in the front seat. Even then, I knew I was not alone. I knew that if God gave me this trial, He would surely not leave me alone in it. I somehow made it home fighting through the tears.

It was 5:15 PM on a hot August day and I had waited all day for the promised phone call. I was driving to my new apartment. Just two days before

I had moved from our house in North Phoenix to a townhouse on Central. It was the second move in just 14 months. My cell phone rang and I hastily pulled out of the busy traffic into a parking lot so I could focus on the words. "Hannah, I need to tell you that you have Stage 3 breast cancer," said the doctor.

Cancer? Stage 3? I was still not prepared to hear those words. I didn't have time for cancer! I longed to go back in time—to be blissfully unaware of the monster growing within. The monster that would change my life forever.

III: The Not So Great Divorce

One-and-a-half years earlier, my husband and I celebrated our 20th wedding anniversary. We went on a special trip to Laguna Beach, California and renewed our vows in a small private ceremony on the beach. During that trip, we talked about moving from our current home in Reading, Pennsylvania to somewhere out West. By the end of the year, we made a decision to move to Arizona. The next six months were a whirlwind of preparing to sell our house, putting it on the market, buying a new house in Phoenix, selling most of our belongings, and packing what remained. By summer we were driving across the country in our caravan of cars and a moving truck.

I have moved a lot in my life. I was born in the Netherlands. My family moved to the United States when I was five years old. I grew up in New Jersey.

After I was married, we lived in several homes in New Jersey, Connecticut, and Pennsylvania. I always thought of our moves positively. I like change and adventure. But moving still creates loss and stress. We had to figure out life in a new place and make new friends. By the end of the year, we had settled in our new home in Phoenix and adjusted to the desert climate. I had figured out shopping, schooling for our four boys, applied for my nursing license and landed in a new church.

"Today's trial is tomorrow's testimony." That's some alliteration. I was scrolling on my phone one morning and took a screenshot of those words. That was the day my husband moved out. Two weeks prior to that, he had dropped the truth bomb that our marriage was not what I thought it was. He had been unfaithful. It rocked my world. I really believed in the "till death do us part" bit of our vows. We had only been living in Arizona for a little over six months.

To be honest, we had not been in sync since I had been ill with bacterial meningitis eight years before. It took me about 18 months to rehabilitate from brain trauma from this infection that nearly killed me. It had absorbed all of my physical and emotional energy. I was a different person as a result of the brain injury. I was on survival mode, not my usual giving mode. And the little bit I had to give went to my four young boys. As we looked back, we both saw that some of the marriage breakdowns occured in that time period. I also recognize that I cannot take the blame for my physical and mental inability when my body was so broken. At least half of people who contract bacterial meningitis die from it. Physically, I came out of it with some minor hearing loss, an imbalance that caused dizziness, and some vision changes. Mentally and emotionally, I was also altered. I lost my driver's license for six months. For that same time period, I had to have a nanny help me do normal life tasks. I lost my autonomy, my control, and who I *had* been. I had to stop working my part-time job as a nurse at a surgery center. In a real sense, it was the beginning of the end of our marriage.

As I look back now, I understand it was also a spiritual battle—the enemy taking advantage of a target. This life is just one giant spiritual battle of good versus evil. *Star Wars* and *The Lord of the Rings* have it right. But I also know my God has *already* won the war, although we still experience the daily battles. Satan wants to pull as many into his army as he can. One of his favorite ways to do this is to go after us with lies. He lies to us with fear, and he manipulates us with discontent and unbelief. He whispers, "The grass is greener on the other side." It's not. The grass is green in your own fields when you stay in them and water them—when you actually work on your problems together. That's what therapy and church community are for. I learned many of these lessons after the fact. I tried to salvage what we had in our marriage. That's the hard part. There are many things I would change and redo if I could. Hindsight is always clearer. You learn so many lessons *from* the pain, but not so many *in* it. Divorce was never in my vocabulary. I never considered it as an option or a part of my future. I learned through my loss how much God had woven loyalty into the fabric of my being. Because I love deeply, I also hurt deeply.

After the divorce, my sense of abandonment was extreme. I had put my hope and trust in my husband all of those years. My hope was seriously misdirected. My hope and trust needed to be in God alone, with my husband doing the same. I realize my ideas about marriage were not how God designed it to be. Marriage is literally serving each other like Jesus models with His church. *That is being One*. It is selfless. Real love is giving, not just taking. And it's certainly not going off somewhere else looking to be gratified. The greatest sadness in my life is my broken marriage because it had a spiraling impact on my children. Sin affects everything. It keeps undoing. It keeps hurting. The effects are unending. Proverbs 19:3 (NLT) says, "People ruin their lives by their own foolishness and then are angry at the Lord." And so my prayer became, "Forgive me; save me from my foolishness." And God reminded me, "Everyone who calls on the name of the Lord will be saved." That is His promise. I certainly could not blame Him for my sin or for my husband's sin choices. Through the loss of my marriage, God faithfully redeemed me on a daily basis. He taught me, step by step, to trust Him fully. On the day that my marriage began to unravel and when it finally ended in divorce, He was my Stronghold.

Going through a separation while getting diagnosed with cancer forced me to navigate the "how" and "what" of my future. I was on an emotional roller coaster of hurt and hope. I felt constantly dashed against the rocks of my husband's despair and the loss of his faith and hope. It was difficult maneuvering through the minefield of emotions exploding on every side. I began to slowly fix my eyes Upward. I was undone. My marriage was imploding. I couldn't fix anything. I tried. I texted. I offered to go to therapy together. There was no way of going back. Just forward. Alone. But not really alone. With God.

We would officially be divorced seven weeks after I first heard the words "You have cancer." Within a few months, I lost parts of my body and the comfort of a relatively healthy life. My life had changed so much in six months that I hardly recognized myself.

IV: Treatment Choices

I did not want to do chemotherapy and radiation. I have always understood cancer to be an immune system problem. Having been diagnosed with Epstein Barr Virus immediately after my youngest son was born, and surviving Adult Bacterial Meningitis, my immune system had already taken a hit. Poisoning was not the answer, especially before surgery. My options were a lumpectomy or a radical double mastectomy. I was well endowed after breastfeeding my four sons and did not want to be deformed at 43. Having always wanted a reduction, I opted for the mastectomy. The doctor recommended chemo before surgery to reduce the tumor load, but that did not make sense to me before major surgery. I needed a strong, not depleted, immune system to recover.

After some research, I found a local naturopathic medical doctor that did immune-boosting IV therapy. At $1,000 per treatment, that wasn't going to be an option for me. My dear friend and fellow nurse, Karen, suggested I start a GoFundMe web page to solicit donations for treatment. The initial contributions began my journey of alternative IV therapy. I began treatment in September. Soon, through a mutual friend, I found Nicole, my current practitioner. With a brilliant researcher's mind, she offered me even more customized care. Over time, we built a sweet friendship as well.

As I was figuring out who would be a part of my medical team caring for me, I went to every new doctor on the premise that I was interviewing them. As an operating room nurse, I am comfortable with surgeons, which became an advantage while I was going through the process of finding optimal care. Instead of having no knowledge of what was to come and then allowing it all just to happen to me, I approached my illness as a well-researched patient. The doctors actually respected me for it, and we had a really good relationship because of it.

My surgery was planned for October 12. I met my plastic surgeon a few weeks prior to discuss breast reconstruction. A work colleague of mine had reconstructive surgery three years prior, and

she had a terrible experience with expanders,
so I knew I did not want to go that route. I
told my plastic surgeon I wanted immediate
reconstruction. I was certain I did not want to
have two surgeries, especially because I was now
working to support myself and my children.
The plastic surgeon agreed to do immediate
reconstruction, along with the breast surgeon who
would be performing the bilateral mastectomy.

My surgery coincided perfectly with my younger
two boys' fall break. Their dad's mom planned to
pick up all four boys and take them on a trip for the
week I had surgery. My mother planned to come
the day before surgery and stay for nine days to
help me recover. It was exactly what I needed. With
this plan in place, I knew I could proceed.

Surgery #1

The day finally arrived, and my mother drove
me to the hospital. The surgery would occur in an
outpatient surgery center, and I would stay for
one night. I hoped to have my anesthesiologist
prearranged, but none of the anesthesiologists
I worked with at my job were able to be there.
As I put on my gown in the preop area, I felt this
incredible peace. I knew I was in God's hands.
I really wasn't afraid. It felt kind of strange to
be this peaceful. I finally understood the verse
in the Bible that says, "The peace of God, which

surpasses all understanding, will guard your hearts and your minds in Christ Jesus" (Philippians 4:7 ESV). It made me think back to the mug that my sweet friend Keely gave me the week before at my "Goodbye Boobie Party." The inscription read: "Peace. It does not mean to be in a place where there is no noise, trouble or hard work. It means to be in the midst of those things and still be calm in your heart." I still drink my coffee out of it every day that it happens to be clean. I need this same reminder: calm comes from God.

Yes, I actually *did* throw myself a "Goodbye Boobie Party." After all, this was a big deal! So I invited friends from all areas of my life. Two good-natured guys even showed up with their wives. It was fun getting my friends to meet each other. I felt their love and support so much during those days. My community was and still is an integral part of my life. I do not take them for granted.

The surgeon came into my little cubicle and drew his purple marker all over my chest to show incision lines. Just before surgery, you typically meet the anesthesiologist as well. To my surprise, a doctor walked in that I actually knew! He was a younger anesthesiologist I had worked with several times. We had a good rapport. He gave me the exact medications I asked for. As an operating room nurse, I knew way too much about what to expect and did not want to remember anything. I

felt safe and well cared for. My last memory from
before surgery is being wheeled down the hallway,
and my next memory is being wheeled to my room.
I do not recall waking up in the recovery room. I
mostly do not want to recall my one night in the
hospital. After my mom went home for the night,
no one checked in on me until I finally yelled loud
enough to get their attention. Post-mastectomy,
moving your arms is very difficult and painful, and
the call button was out of reach. I used the pain
pump regularly and finally and very painfully got
myself up to the bathroom at some point. As soon
as I could go home, I did. I was in the hospital for
less than 24 hours. I wanted my own food and bed.
My mom responded to me with the attention I
needed much more quickly than a floor nurse ever
could.

Recovery

Initially, post-mastectomy, my life was all about
positioning and getting as comfortable as possible.
I literally needed five pillows to sleep. I was not
allowed to lay on my side and everything hurt if
it wasn't supported. Nobody warns you about the
discomfort that comes with such radical surgery.
"Take the pain medication," I told myself. As much
as I like to be the "natural girl," this was not the
time for heroics. My biggest issue was not any pain
in my chest, it was the nerve endings that were on

fire. All the breast tissue had been removed, and my nerve endings didn't know where they began or ended. It was the beginning of about six weeks of intense burning, numbness, and itching. I had not read anything in the literature about this. Clothing on the back of my arms or near the top of my chest hurt, which left me with limited options. My life began to be centered on physical comfort.

I was actually pleasantly surprised immediately after surgery when I first saw my new breasts. Although scarred, they fit my body. Later, my plastic surgeon said he and the representative in the operating room had chosen the size to match my body. I knew I still had many months of healing ahead of me, but I already felt happier than I had been in a while.

Once the mothers left, I had to renegotiate my entire life. I could no longer chop carrots, lift my cast iron pans, or close my car trunk. My boys were a huge help to me. They went food shopping with me. They helped me cook, and they helped with laundry. It was a time to bond as well as teach. I homeschooled them up until that school year, and now here was a chance to teach my boys the chores they needed to really learn for life. It had been a year of great change for our family. I did not know then that I would be working full-time the following year. I would come to rely heavily on their help to keep our home running smoothly.

As independent as I had become in the past year as a single mother, I began feeling the loss of that post surgery. I was at the mercy of the guy at the cash register to help put the groceries in the car. I had to rely on just about everyone around me to help get all life's mundane tasks done. It was humbling. It brought me to a place of dependence, not only on those around me but on God. I had nowhere else to go. It brought me back to eight months before, when I had essentially been abandoned by my husband. The feelings of deep loneliness, sadness, and regret had been overwhelming. But God didn't let me wallow in that. I'm still amazed at the strength He gave me in those initial months. Through my new diagnosis, surgery, and recovery, He showed me that the strength within me came from Him. All along, He was carrying me. It reminded me of that poem *Footprints* where there are two sets of footprints in the sand, and then all of a sudden there was only one set of footprints. At first glance it looks like abandonment, and then comes the realization you were being carried. It was a beautiful picture to me. I was not alone. I had never been alone, even in the darkest days of my marriage, the darkest days of my separation, and the darkest days after my diagnosis and surgery.

I was getting a glimpse of the "why" of the trial I was in. I knew I would never fully understand it all, but this experience helped me step back and look at my life with a perspective I never had before. It was like God put me out into the universe and showed me the big picture. Sometimes that step back is the hardest step to take. It is the greatest trial to go through, but it brings the sweetest peace.

V: BACK TO WORK

My first job out of nursing school at age 21 was at an eye surgery center in New Jersey that performed cataract and corneal eye surgery. I worked with the top ten eye surgeons in Northern New Jersey and was trained to both circulate and scrub (hand surgical instruments) many procedures. It was experience that eventually gave me work in every state I lived in, as there is always a need for eye surgery.

I see how God guided me and provided for me in this way. When we moved to Phoenix, I intended to work as a nurse as soon as I could, but due to a misfiled paper, I waited three months for my nursing license paperwork to transfer from Pennsylvania. Since I had previous surgical assistant training, the center hired me as a surgical technician on a nurse's salary on a per diem basis until my nursing license transferred. This provided just the right timing to develop a relationship with each eye surgeon as a scrub technician handling surgical instruments. Eye surgery is not one of those things you can hack your way through. There is a great deal of trust established between the surgeon and the tech. You learn to anticipate the instrument needed before the surgeon even knows they need it. I was already trained to use a microscope during surgery, which gave me credibility. The surgeons learned to trust me. Eventually several of them offered me jobs. Although I did not accept them, it was a validation to me. One surgeon also ended up being my ticket to Fiji. I had an awesome opportunity to travel with him and a team to serve the people in Fiji by providing eye surgery. It was a life-changing trip for me.

After the mastectomy, which occurred exactly one year after starting my job, I spent over five weeks at home before venturing back to work. Since my job as a circulator in the operating room included intense movements and physical abilities I could not perform, I was unable to resume my normal nursing duties. But the one thing I could do was hand instruments to the surgeons, so I initially spent about three weeks doing this job.

Although I still needed a lot of assistance getting back into my regular job, I became stronger and stronger as I healed from surgery. The work strengthened me physically, and everyone at work was helpful and supportive. At the end of November, my supervisor approached me and asked me to seriously consider working full-time. Our head company was changing the structure of their hiring process and would no longer offer per diem positions. I was basically forced to go full-time or quit. However, having officially divorced two months prior, this was also good timing for me. It gave me the ability to provide medical insurance for my children, as well as short-term disability insurance, paid time off, and other benefits. I accepted the offer.

My parents came to visit for ten days in December. We developed a special bond during this time. They stayed at a timeshare but came over daily to spend time with the boys. They have this amazing ability to organize, and they love to share this gift! Since moving, I had not yet put everything in its place. They structured a little office in my room, made some sense of my walk-in closet, and put the garage in order. It was also the busiest month of work for me that year, so it was wonderful to come home to a home-cooked meal and not worry about laundry or cleaning. God was providing respite through my family.

Christmas and New Year's came and went. As I peered ahead into the expanse of a new year, I wondered. Would I be completely healed? Would I move? What was I going to do? I did not have any answers. But I knew that my Creator did. I was learning to trust Him when I couldn't trust myself—when I didn't know if I was coming or going. I could trust Him when I didn't have enough work for the first few months of the year, even though I was working full time. I could trust Him when I wasn't getting support checks from my ex-husband. I didn't know what the year would hold, but I knew I was safe because He was taking care of me every step of the way.

VI:
RECONNECTIONS

My parents offered to pay my way for a visit to see them in North Carolina in February. It also happened to be the 50th birthday of my oldest sister, Judith. I decided it would be a really fun surprise for her. Her husband and several of her five children knew I was visiting, but she didn't.

A week before my flight, I had a patient with a previous bilateral mastectomy. She was wearing a little cuff on her arm to indicate she was not allowed to have blood pressures or IV done on that arm. Typically, after a mastectomy and lymph node removal, a condition called lymphedema (swelling of the arms or legs) can develop. Somehow we got on the topic, and she encouraged me to find a lymphedema sleeve to wear on the airplane since the altitude change can exacerbate swelling. So I found a double sleeve on Amazon and had it delivered before the trip. I loved how God was taking care of me, even in little ways. He gave me a patient that could help me navigate this whole new world I was living in. Anyone else would call it a coincidence, but these were not happy accidents. These were God moments! I was learning to pay attention to them. They happened all the time. I just needed to open my eyes to them. I was learning to sense the Spirit in my life. He is always present. And I was starting to realize it on a daily basis.

Everything took planning in those days, from what clothes I could wear to the activities I could do. But I finagled my way through it. This wasn't going to alter me forever. For example, putting on the lymphedema sleeve took some practice. It's linked over the shoulder to each arm and was super tight. In order to put it on in the airport bathroom, I could only wear tank tops. I even had to ask for help from strangers to put it on or take it off. I found it was a way to share my story. I was determined to figure things out and live life. I successfully surprised my sister and enjoyed catching up with my family. It had been too long—a time span I did not want to repeat. Sadly, our 2000 mile distance had kept me from being part of their regular lives. I determined to not let this happen again. Family is so important.

After the trip, exercise became a serious focus. I started out jogging and lifting weights in the gym of my condo complex. Soon I started biking. I worked my way up from indoor to outdoor, from three to twenty miles. I felt strong and confident. But I could only squeeze in workouts on the weekends. With my job, I felt like I was already highly active each day. Working as a nurse in the operating room requires strength and stamina. We push beds, move sleeping patients, prep heavy limbs, and are constantly on the move to provide the sterile surgical and anesthesia teams with the items they need throughout the case. I loved my job. As rewarding as it was, the actual job was not stressful, but the long hours were.

Most importantly, it allowed me to provide for myself and my sons, all of whom lived with me. Three out of four were still in high school. Being an OR nurse is a fast-paced, demanding job requiring one to be on their feet most of the day. I woke up every morning while it was still dark to get to work. I relied heavily on the help of my sons to keep our home running smoothly. I needed to keep up my health and energy to work full time while fighting Stage 3 cancer. I was working 40-hour weeks on top of receiving long IV treatments three times per week. I had to work to keep my life and kids afloat. I could feel myself burning the candle at both ends and didn't know how to blow either side out.

Jones

I received a phone call from an old friend I'd known in my teens and twenties. He was grieving a death in his family and his broken marriage. This man was in deep pain—pain I knew only too well. To protect his identity, I will call him Jones. I came up with this nickname because he reminded me of Indiana Jones. He had traveled the world and collected artifacts. The name suited his adventurous spirit—a spirit I grew to love.

Over the next few weeks, we kept in touch via text. We had always enjoyed a witty banter, and somehow that translated into our texts. It was fun. It was lively. It was making me laugh like I had not laughed in months, maybe years. It was healing laughter. Jones was a friend who understood my pain, as I understood his. We had a deep emotional connection. He let me in. He cared for me in my insecurity and pain, and he let me safely open my wounded heart. He allowed me to be real and share my heart.

We had eight months of long-distance friendship living thousands of miles apart, enduring and processing the heartache we both felt from the loss of our previous relationships. We could identify with one another like no one else could in our lives. We envisioned a future together full of friendship. We enjoyed many of the same things, such as skiing and water activities. We talked for hours each day via Facetime, and he fell asleep to me reading practically the same chapter of a C.S. Lewis book we shared every night over the phone. But it would not be forever.

VII: Changing Course

Nearly a year after my double mastectomy, my cancer treatment and monitoring were ongoing. My October 2 CT scan results were concerning. All of a sudden my body was showing new nodal activity. My armpit nodes had grown and several new lymph nodes in my chest and lung appeared. Nicole, my nurse practitioner, suggested I see a pulmonary specialist at the Mayo Clinic. I saw him on October 9. Christi, nurse colleague of mine, insisted on coming along. Her sister had been through lung cancer and had been treated by the Mayo.

The doctor at the Mayo Clinic tested me for Valley Fever, an infection often found in the Phoenix valley from spores in the air. My test came back negative. I had to figure out what the new changes in my body were. We scheduled a PET scan for October 16. I worked that day and had the scan after work. The results were expected the following day. Overnight, I developed a migraine and in the morning I called in sick to work. My mind was not going to be on my patients that day. The doctor called and informed me that the PET scan results showed all of the areas lit up. This was either due to infection or cancer. My specialist encouraged me to have a biopsy done at the Mayo Clinic.

The results of the biopsy showed that my original diagnosis had changed from HER2+ to HER2-, which meant that I now had a completely different type of protien growth factor. This significantly changed my treatment protocol possibilities. The oncologist at the Mayo Clinic wanted to bring my results before the tumor board since she wasn't 100% certain on what my treatment protocol should be. It took over a week to hear back from her, so in the meantime, I saw another oncologist recommended by Nicole, who made herself available to come along to this appointment. I wanted to get another opinion since my test results were ambivalent.

An older doctor walked into the room. After his review of my case, he felt strongly that I was HER2+ and wanted to put me through the biggest chemotherapy regime he had. He actually scared me a little. Again, my heart was saying, "No, get another opinion." During that week, two people in my life had mentioned the Cancer Treatment Centers of America. (After the fact, I started realizing that God was nudging me through other people echoing and repeating similar things.) I was able to make an appointment for the week of Thanksgiving. The Cancer Treatment Centers of America have an intensive evaluation process that takes three days. This includes doing blood work, meeting with an entire team of practitioners, and coming up with a personalized treatment protocol.

Jones came into town on the Sunday before Thanksgiving. I wanted to get a tattoo on my wrist that said "live" in lowercase cursive. We went to a nice tattoo place in Scottsdale. The tattoo took all of 5 minutes to get and felt like a skewer was scraping me. But every day since, as I put on my bracelets, I see this word that is so special to me and reminds me to value the breath I wake up with, take the chance I have to see the sunrise, and hug my boys. It's my reminder to use each day well.

My results were expected on Friday, the day after Thanksgiving. Jones made a huge effort to drive back from visiting family to be there for me when I received my new treatment plan for my metastatic cancer diagnosis. He made a point to be there in person for me. As we sat listening to the oncologist's recommendation to take oral medication, we kept looking at each other incredulously! What?! I was totally expecting to start chemotherapy the following Monday. I couldn't believe it. I had been prepared for the worst, but instead, I was given another chance.

In a very real way, Jones was a life-line to me during thet difficult first year of fighting breast cancer. We talked via video chat during my three-hour intravenous vitamin C treatments, making the time fly. He flew me out for visits. We had amazing adventures together. He spoiled me with an entire new wardrobe for my birthday—new clothes for my new body. He was a gift from God.

I expected Jones and myself to go forward with our future together. But over the next month, God made it apparent that He had other plans for me. As he drifted away emotionally, I knew that I needed to give him the space he was creating and break our relationship.

I was still putting my trust in people and the stuff of life. At the time I could not understand this part of my story. How could a relationship end so abruptly? Perhaps Jones could not be simultaneously present for my pain and his own. He played a huge part in helping me handle my diagnosis and kept me laughing when I could have easily turned to tears and sorrow. He played the earthly hero in my story. He is gifted to help the hurting, which is a beautiful, laughter-filled gift.

But the greater story is about my Heavenly Hero, and how I fell in love with Him. It's the story of redemption, forgiveness, and a loving Father who cares for His child no matter how many times she screws up and makes mistakes. She isn't perfect—far from it. She tries not to make her life look too put together on social media. That is not real. Life is raw. It's definitely unpredictable. But it's also so incredibly and beautifully choreographed by the Creator that it sometimes does seem almost unreal. God was revealing a new plan for me, one that would teach me to lean into Him for everything. I had been putting a lot of my joy in my friend—a bit misplaced and misappropriated. Yet God knew this was my time to turn to Him for my everything.

I cannot lie—I felt abandoned by yet another man. The pain cut deep. It broke my heart into a million pieces. I cried for weeks. The abrupt end of our relationship felt like a death. But it taught me a lesson I had yet to learn—the lesson of not trusting in man. And I don't mean "a man." I mean not putting *all* my hope in a person to give me joy and peace. I had fantastic fun with my friend, but he couldn't meet my deepest need. I needed peace and true hope in a Father and Husband that would never fail me. God was using my broken pieces to make me new and build me into a strong, empowered woman of God. Looking back, I can see God's supernatural hand in all of it. He wanted my worship. He kindly redirected my heart back to

Him. He gently removed Jones from my life, and over the course of time has been healing that loss of friendship. Even when it hurts, even when I feel the ache of rejection and abandonment, I have to trust Him. I'm learning in this life that God is faithful, and He will not abandon me. Not ever.

VIII: Stage 4—
The Stage I
Never Planned
to Be On

The amazing part of having a life-altering disease is the vast amount of knowledge you gain. From diagnosis on, I was in full-on research mode. There were weeks I spent at least an hour a day researching. I wanted, no, *needed*, to understand what was happening to me. Initially, I educated myself on Stage 3 cancer. What IDC meant. What ER/PR was. What HER2 status involved. What in the world was *high grade*? These terms were all new to me. As a nurse, I had never been involved in the cancer part of healthcare. Stage 3 meant that my cancer lump in my breast was a certain size, but there was also involvement in my armpit lymph nodes. My original diagnosis was ER/PR+ and HER2+ and high grade, so it was fast-growing and "triple positive," or hormone positive.

A part of my alternative treatment protocol was mega doses of intravenous vitamin C as well as other vitamins, minerals, and supplements. Over the course of time, my left arm veins began to collapse and scar. We realized it was time to get a port-a-cath implanted in my chest wall to make it easier to receive IV treatments three times a week. This was surgery #2. Thankfully, it was a pretty easy same-day procedure, and I was able to plan ahead and get one of my favorite anesthesiologists to be there for the surgery.

Part of my self-initiated treatment protocol was to get CT scans every three months to see whether my IV treatments were working. From November to June, in 8 months, the tiny lymph nodes in my armpits and lungs shrunk. (There is a whole other story I could tell as an aside. I realize now that I was likely misdiagnosed and was probably Stage 4 from the beginning, due to lung involvement, but my doctors never did a scan before surgery as a baseline.) The October CT scan unexpectedly showed a bunch of new activity in lymph nodes in my upper chest, next to my trachea, as well as my lungs.

All of a sudden it got real. I felt out of control. After that PET scan and biopsy of the paratracheal lymph node (surgery #3) at the Mayo, my cancer diagnosis changed from HER2+ to HER2-, and I went with the treatment protocol recommended by the doctor affiliated with the Cancer Treatment Centers of America. Once again, I was faced with surgery in a new setting with an OR team that I did not know, but once again, in walked an anesthesiologist I already knew and trusted! I ended up with four surgeries in the time span of 16 months. At every single surgery, in four different hospitals all over the Phoenix valley, I had an anesthesiologist take care of me that I personally knew and had worked with. That's not a coincidence! God kept quieting some of my biggest fears.

Metastatic breast cancer (or Stage 4) is incurable by definition. The need to prioritize my health caused me to pull away from the demands of work. At the time, I was not receiving any child support from my ex-husband and I had no idea how I was going to survive financially without full-time work, but my story shows how God takes care of His children. I knew that I needed to focus on my health and treatment, so I filed for Social Security Disability (which takes six months to begin receiving), filed for FMLA at work (Family Medical Leave Act, which protects your job for eight weeks or more) and Short Term Disability (an income insurance covering about 80% of my salary that I had deducted from my paycheck since I had started full-time work). I first received a phone call informing me I had qualified for Short Term Disability. I was ecstatic. I knew that at least my basic income needs were covered for now. I could take a break from my everyday crazy work schedule and focus on my new life and "job" as a patient. My updated treatment protocol was an oral medication therapy. I had prepared myself for IV chemotherapy and was pleasantly shocked to find out I did not need to lose my hair! I began researching this treatment and began the process of shutting down my ovaries the following month. My cancer was hormone-driven so I needed to stop estrogen from feeding it. Along with this injection, I began an oral estrogen blocker and a targeted therapy called IBRANCE®. It was a CDK 4/6 Inhibitor that worked on the second phase of the cell cycle. With this new chance came side effects: intense fatigue and changes in appetite, skin, and hair. Initially, it wiped me out. God provided comfort in the form of a dog. Zed. My therapy dog. He is the best snuggler in the world. He got me outside! He licked my tears.

IX: A Chorus of Friends

My chorus of friends has been truly astounding. At the beginning of my journey, it was my family: my parents, my mom-in-law, my two sisters, my brother- and sister-in-law, and my four beautiful boys. Then it was my small group. My mentor Ann. Sweet ladies in my church. Girlfriends from out east. My cousin in Holland. Brigette. Jones. And my new bestie, Sara. God was building a hedge about me. They were His hands, His feet, His mouth, His arms around me. It became a beautiful reminder and lesson to me of why we need community, and why we need to become vulnerable sometimes. This was *their* chance to serve Him by serving me. In my moments of sorrow, loneliness, and grief, these people showed up and loved me like Jesus.

Brigette, My 40-Year-Old Vinny

Where to begin with Brigette? Although I'm introducing her so late in the story, she was an integral friend through my divorce, my diagnosis, and my healing. Years earlier, to share my interest in food and healthy eating, I started a Facebook page highlighting my food and recipes. Brigette and I met on a Paleo food Facebook page, and she started following me. One day she sent me a private message asking for advice on her diet. We started getting to know each other and quickly realized we were both Christians. She had also been divorced and had children around my kids' ages. She was close to my age, we ate almost identically, and she was a colon cancer survivor. And she became my very best friend. (You may notice I have many best friends! Someone once gave me permission to have many best friends. They can each have a role in your life in different ways.) She was also my best pen pal. We had known each other for several years and still had never met in person. At first, we only messaged on Facebook. Then we started to text. We talked every day, all day. My friends started calling her my 40-year-old Vinny. I mean, she *could* just be a creep pretending to be a 40-year-old female! So Brigette and I made plans to finally meet each other.

My plane landed in Portland, Oregon, and I took a shuttle bus to meet Brigette in the town where she worked. It was such a sweet meeting. I got off the bus, and we just ran into each other's arms crying. She knew me as no other person did at the time. There's something about texting someone and feeling the safety to pour out your heart, bare your soul, and show your real self. And she loved me for it. For myself. The real me. I think our friends and family thought we were crazy and gave a collective sigh of relief that our friendship worked in person, too. We joked that if we didn't get along, we could always just sit next to each other and text.

We ate and talked, and she shared her family and town with me. We enjoyed so many of the same things. Girlfriend things: coffee and shopping, Netflix binging (we actually watched the same shows while apart), fashion, good food, cooking, movies, our kids, and obsessing over our health, to name a few. We often wished we lived next door to each other. We'd make great neighbors. She'd be the Ethel to my Lucy. We developed a deep bond that seemed to be exactly what we both needed for that season.

My East Coast Girlfriend Tour

God put on my heart a plan to take a trip. In February, I headed east for my first stop: my "East Coast Girlfriend Tour." I grew up on the East Coast and lived in three different states over 35 years. I had accumulated a lot of good friendships. There was a deep pull to reconnect with these women. My East Coast Girlfriend Tour lasted 12 days, and I saw 25 of my dear friends. And these were just a few of my favorite East Coast ones who were available to see me! When a friend at home heard this number, she mentioned she didn't even *have* that many girlfriends! God so blessed me with these beautiful friendships. They became the joys and silver linings of moving so often. And it was the beginning of learning to share my God story.

Holland, Hillsong, and Hope

My second stop was Holland! Although I was born there, it had been 20 years since I had last visited. Because my parents were going, and it was my cousin's 25th wedding anniversary, it seemed like a good opportunity to go. I searched for flights and found airline tickets that landed me in Holland only an hour after my parents planned to arrive. God paved the way! During the five hour flight to Holland through Iceland, I found myself sitting next to Peter, an older gentleman and a professor from Germany. I had the chance to tell him my story of God's amazing grace and healing. It was the beginning of a greater inspiration to not only tell my story, but to write it down.

My trip to Holland connected me back to my roots. I lived in Holland until I was almost six years old, and I returned every year until I was 18. I became engaged to be married there at 20 years old, and the last trip had been with my six-month-old firstborn son, Liam. Twenty years is a long time! I spent time with both sides of my family. My mom is one of 12, and my dad is the oldest of seven siblings. I have over 75 first cousins! I was able to stay with my cousin Durvina and her beautiful family. We biked the paths of southern Holland, wandered the cobbled streets of the old towns of my youth, and enjoyed the delights of Dutch treats. It was an adventure! One evening I reconnected with aunts and uncles over a family dinner. Another afternoon, I gathered with a group of my female cousins. These girls had prayed for me as a group on several occasions during my cancer journey. We had a time of communion and hands-on prayer which moved my spirit. In several months prior to this, I experienced other occasions of hands-on prayer. My elders and church leaders came over to my house the month after I was first diagnosed with cancer and prayed over me. This kind of Spirit-led prayer is a powerful experience. As I look back, these were the moments I knew and felt God's presence. I was learning to listen, to pay attention, to hear His promptings.

The day after our cousin gathering, my cousin Hester flew me to London to attend a women's conference. My first Hillsong Colour Conference was the next step in the revival of my soul. There was such a profound sense of the Holy Spirit's presence in the singing of over 11,000 women.

These major "wow" moments on earth give me a tiny glimpse of what heaven must be like.

I started to recognize God writing a story in my life, especially in small moments that reorient me to Him. For example, I chatted with my seat-mate on our tiny jet flight to London. The next day, as I walked through the stadium filled to the brim with 11,000 women, this same girl literally grabbed my hand. And we were also on the same flight home a few days later. All things are perfectly orchestrated. God is in the details of our lives. I'm in His hands, and His Spirit is in me.

I first heard Bobbie Houston preach at this conference. She challenged me to think about my life. She asked, "How do I love Him?" The answer was not by screaming at the life that I was now experiencing. And, boy, I sure could scream at this point! I lost my breasts, my husband, my best friend, what I thought was financial security, my health ... I could go on and on. The answer? The way we love God is by learning to lean into Him. She reminded me that He gave us the Holy Spirit to comfort and convict us. When we wrap ourselves with His strength, His power, and His grace, we can move forward in life, past the hurt, the pain, the illness, and the injury to a place of peace, smothered with His Spirit kiss divine (James 4:8). How do we do this? By really knowing what He says about who He is and who we are in Him. We need to read His love letter to us, His word. This is how we are transformed, as our minds are renewed by His word.

The Chorus Grows

When we surround ourselves with a chorus of friends filled with His truth, His wisdom, and His Holy Spirit, we sing the song of salvation together and link arms on our journey through this Earth. We need community. We need to be rooted and planted where we stand so when the waves of difficulty of life threaten to overwhelm us, we know we are not alone. We know whose we are. I need a *faith* community. We all do. God gives us community (even if it's family) to *speak truth* and *testify* to what is real and what Jesus says. There's no going it alone. As my pastor, Frank, says, "Christianity is a team sport."

1 Corinthians 1:10 says, "I urge you, my brothers and sisters, for the sake of the name of our Lord Jesus Christ, to agree to live in unity with one another and put to rest any division that attempts to tear you apart. Be restored as one united body living in perfect harmony. *Form a consistent choreography* among yourselves, having a common perspective with shared values." This is the Church! I love the concept of choreography. Together. It's not always synchronous, but there is blending, moving, coming together at times, side by side at

times, and apart at times. We are a choreography always realigning towards Heaven.

Hebrews 12:1 says, "As for us, we have all of these great witnesses who encircle us like clouds. So we must let go of every wound that has pierced us and the sin we so easily fall into. Then we will be able to run life's marathon race with passion and determination, for the path has already been marked out before us." This is a call to forgiveness, even when it is hard and the hurt runs so very deep. Every wound. Not just the little easy ones.

My chorus of friends continues to grow. It now includes unsuspecting writers like Bobbie Houston and Lisa Bevere, who have been used by God to make a huge impact on my understanding of my calling as a woman. Reconnections with family in Holland are part of my chorus. New friends I made waiting in line at a conference have become texting buddies and major prayer warriors across the miles!

And Linda! I cannot fail to mention her. Often one of the sad tragedies of broken marriages is losing family. Instead of pushing me away, my in-laws wrapped their hearts around me in my pain. My ex-husband's sister-in-law, Linda, and I bonded as my losses accumulated. She became my prayer warrior and confidante, speaking truth and love into my life. As she was hearing God and learning to recognize His voice, she shared her desire to help others tell their God-stories and became the editing voice of my story. (She's not allowed to touch this paragraph though!)

And now, I recognize I have a role as part of this chorus. God is calling me to create a Sisterhood in our church. It's there in small bits, but we are working toward a collective, cohesive group of ladies of all ages, ethnicities, and backgrounds. We need relationship! I mean, I know I do! I believe the Spirit is leading me for this purpose. A dear friend encouraged me to open my home as a first step. "Invite whoever will come." So I planned a potluck breakfast. I have this gorgeous home with a huge living space and an incredible antique table from my parents that extends to seat 12. About 20 beautiful ladies showed up with amazing food! We spent two hours in fellowship, getting to know one another. There was no Bible study or homework. We just talked. We recognized the need to go deeper, to minister to one another, to encourage. I was blessed by a particular conversation with an older woman wherein I confessed my struggles as a single mom. I told her how I felt like I lacked in the ability to be a spiritual leader to my four sons. Since then, she has encouraged me so much! I often find that the Spirit speaks to us through His people. Words of truth. Words of comfort. Words of encouragement.

Another time, I talked with Tina, a friend from church. In the context of how my low immune function was keeping me from serving, I said, "It's so hard to have these gifts and abilities and skills and not be able to use them in the way that I think I need to. I know God can use me, I just need to ask Him to show me how. These are the moments I hate stupid cancer and how it's wrecked so much of my life. But I *know* He makes beauty out of the ashes. I cling to that." Tina encouraged me with her experience: "I think when I've been wrecked the most is when He's totally done the beautiful and unexpected things in my life! We need to believe and cling to His promises!"

I feel this great calling on my life now to encourage, testify, and grow communities of women. We need to speak truth into one another's lives. We need this Sisterhood. When I came home from a visit with friends in Cincinnati, I had an Uber driver pick me up late at night from the airport. Her name was Joann and, after a few sentences, we recognized our shared faith. When we got to my house, she got my suitcase out of the trunk and prayed over me!

The day I found out my Income Disability got revoked, I was flying back home to Arizona from a trip to Pennsylvania. Due to my cancer diagnosis, I always opted out of the airport scanner and received a pat-down. This beautiful older black woman named Bessie was the TSA agent that started the pat-down. She sensed my spirit and began quoting bible verses as she started on my head and arms. It was POWERFUL and I knew she was there to remind me to trust Him. I bawled my way to my gate in gratitude. He places His people everywhere! We have an amazing opportunity to encourage each other and remind each other that we are not alone.

Sara

After my divorce was final, I started praying for a best friend to share life with. The difficulty of moving often and changing states is the sad reality of leaving friends behind. I was feeling this void in my life. I specifically prayed for someone close to my age. And God provided Sara. Not only was she the same age (she was only one day older than me!) she was recently divorced, and a new believer in Jesus. My two years of friendship with her were mingled with joy and sorrow.

"Han, I want to have faith like yours. You wear your faith like it's your skin." These were the words of my best friend. Sara was an extremely significant part of my daily life for two of the most difficult years of my life. She was the person God used to teach me how to put words to my faith—to literally put skin to my faith. Not only was I living out my faith for her to see in the middle of loss and brokenness, but I was also investing my heart into *her* brokenness and pain. I think of the term "skin in the game" and recognize the risk we incur when we enter into another's life, into the hard stuff. God compelled me to "go all-in" with her, to be His voice to her from a place of understanding and true unconditional love. I did not do this perfectly, but I loved her deeply.

I'm using past tense because I have to. My sweet beautiful friend took her life just two short years after I met her. Losing her so unexpectedly was one of the saddest days of my life. During my divorce, I asked God for a friend. I had older friends, younger friends, married friends, and friends far away. But I didn't have a local friend who was my age. God provided Sara! We texted all day, every day, and spent almost every other weekend together when her children were away with their dad. Those two years were mingled with laughter and deeply-felt tears for her. Her sense of humor made us burst out in peals of laughter, yet our combined tears could fill pools. Psalm 56:8 says, "You've kept track of all my wandering and my weeping. You've stored my many tears in your bottle—not one will be lost." Sara and I joked that God was collecting our tears in an Olympic-sized pool, not a bottle! We recognized what a gift we were to each other. We gave each other hugs and knew it was God's arms. We prayed over each other. We asked each other the hard questions we couldn't always ask another person. There are few people in our lives we can be 100% real and open with. Sara was this for me, and I believe I was for her.

Sara: *What does it mean to surrender to Him [God]?*

Hannah: *Giving the situation and struggle with it TO Him. It doesn't mean giving it up. It means being a strong Warrior Mom standing with your Perfect Advocate. It's not giving anything "up" but handing it over to Him and letting Him use you as Warrior Mom while He surrounds you with His Angel Armies and indwells you with His SPIRIT!! How cool is that? That is how it all works. Jesus, give me words. Jesus, transform my thinking, my life, my all. Use me. Help me reflect YOU.*

Sara: *Love! Going to read it and dwell on things you write... So in my situation... also trust and "be still?"*

Hannah: *In EVERY situation. It doesn't always mean "do nothing." It means "to rest in Him." It means ask Him to show you EXACTLY what to do, how to do it. Look for His guidance. Apply His wisdom. You get that from reading His word and counsel.*

Sara asked many questions, often as we texted, and it challenged me to put words to what God was teaching me and helping me to learn. Sara and I had both been through sad divorces. We were struggling with "losing control of our lives" and the plans we had for the future. The future was supposed to be rosy, not this sad! And definitely not this lonely!

Sara: *This is a random question ... Allison was saying how one would not know or feel their sin unless the Holy Spirit was within them. Is that based on faith?*

Hannah: *I think she meant "feel the weight of their sin" - that is what Jesus died for. It's based on His mercy really, that He calls you Child. Your faith is a gift from Him. You believe because He chose you. Before the foundations of the world were even put into motion. That's how amazing His love is for you.*

Sara: *Okay going deeper. We believe because He chose us, so is being saved or is salvation, the time when we turned our lives to Jesus and were forgiven? And for others, were they not chosen, hence, do not believe?*

Hannah: *Yes, and yes. But we don't get to know who they are (on this side of heaven) so we are called to reflect Him to the world. I think that this transformation starts to happen when you recognize your need of Him and repent and turn from your sin (but you have been chosen since before you were born.) So it's NOTHING that YOU DO that saves you. But because of His gift of grace for us to believe, we SHOULD live a life of obedience to Him and share Him. The very understanding that He chose you should give you TREMENDOUS confidence in Him, in His plan for you, in His great Love for you!!*

Sara: *Yes!! (This is good book material. lol) … one more, can't anyone be saved?*

Hannah: *Anyone can be that was chosen. He wrote our story before we were ever born. For His glory.*

Sara knew I was writing a book. She was the one who gave me the title. She gave me the idea. Her plan was to be my book tour coordinator. She would always joke about it. So these are very difficult things for me to write about.

There is so much discomfort and sadness with suicide. There are feelings and thoughts that say, "I should have…" or "I could have…" But I was reminded by my friend Allison, on that tragic day, that I was not Sara's "Redeemer" or "Savior." My job had been Encourager. Friend. Hugger. I pointed her up to her Lord even when life was hard. He was the lifter of her head. I got to be in her life to remind her. I couldn't fix the depression or anxiety. But I could and did keep directing her to the One that does. It's still difficult to comprehend it all. Why does God allow such pain? It was the *fifth* great loss of my life in under four years. But I learned this: God wasn't asking me to fix Sara. My function in her life was to encourage her, to help build her faith despite her difficulties while watching me learn in mine. And in all of that, He was building my faith and teaching me who He is. My Healer. My Provider. My Sustainer. My Peace.

He was emptying me out so I could be filled with Him. His Spirit was pouring into me and filling me to overflowing. My wrap-around God comforted me with His massive arms. In the midst of great loss, I had great peace.

Do I miss her? Yes. Every day. But I also have such great joy knowing she is at rest in her Savior's arms. She is not crying and sad anymore, and that is so awesome!

Sara*: You are doing it and stronger than I.*

Hannah: *Strong in Him. We are all on different steps in our journey. Don't compare. We link arms to Heaven girl. Sometimes pulling and sometimes being pulled. But always moving forward. Perfection is in Heaven. You're gonna screw up all the way there. It's BELIEVING He is actually writing a WAY better story for us than we ever could!*

X: Breaking Up with Me

In a one year span, I lost two of the very best friends I had ever had. The pain of it was raw. Yet He was calling me to surrender it all. I see it in the screenshots of quotes I saved that year. Even though I wasn't truly understanding the depth and emptying I was going to experience at the time, it was a merciful, systematic, slow process of breaking down my strongholds, one at a time.

My Job Years

In the Bible, Job loses everything—his children, his reputation, his health. He asks God a lot of the same questions I asked, but I had not quite spoken them in audible words. As I read through Job, I related to his story and held on to the same truths:

"But he knows where I am going. And when he tests me, I will come out as pure as gold" (Job 23:10 NLT)

"The Almighty himself will be your treasure. He will be your precious silver!" (Job 22:25 NLT)

I began to see my suffering as God's divine act of mercy, changing my "old thinking" perspective of faith into a real understanding of what faith in God is or should be. Faith is not just based on what He did and does, but on who He is.

God taught me through His word, saying, *"You can go through a day without the fear of stumbling when you walk in the One who gives light to the world. But you will stumble when the light is not in you, for you'll be walking in the dark"* (John 11:10).

I found a promise for me in how Jesus viewed Lazarus, his very dear friend, who was dying. *"This sickness will not end in death for Lazarus, but will bring glory and praise to God. This will reveal the greatness of the Son of God by what takes place"* (John 11:4). What a shift in thinking! This isn't really about me at all! It's about Him! I get to glorify Him in my "sickness" and point everyone UP. My body may die, but I have great hope and confidence in living forever. This life isn't all about my needs. It is all about serving Him and praising Him while led by His Holy Spirit.

Somehow, the role and person of the Holy Spirit in my understanding of living by faith was greatly lacking. I guess the churches I attended in the past didn't teach much about Him, or I didn't pay attention. But wow! The reality of the Holy Spirit was another huge thing God was teaching me. I was waking up! Revival was in my heart!

Grace is not a thing, but a person—the Holy Spirit. He makes us His home. How cool is that? Romans 8:6 says, *"For the mind-set of the flesh is death, but the mind-set controlled by the Spirit finds life and peace."* I am learning to hear His voice more and more.

The Massive Spiritual Battle For My Worship

We all worship something all the time. We worship whatever we give the most important place in our priorities and affections. My ever-present question started to become, "To whom am I giving my worship?" God? Or all the stuff of this world (which means NOT God, which means Satan). My health, my comfort, and feeling loved by a man had become the most important things to me—my idols. These are not inherently bad things, but they became my supreme focus, instead of my Creator who is actually my Healer, Sustainer, and Provider.

There are two lies we often believe: "I can't come to God because I'm so awful," or "I don't go to God because I don't think I need Him." But the opposite is true; you do need Him.

He's your Creator. God loves you more than anyone. He knows you. He knows your every need and your every thought. He has paved the way for you to Himself and heaven by sending Jesus. He died in your place so that you don't have to go to hell for your sin. He did that so you can know peace and have eternal life forever. Don't put your hope in your feelings. Some days are going to feel really bad, but they don't change His promises to you. He is always faithful, even when we aren't. Faith is a gift from God. Just ask Him for it. It's not based on how you are feeling on a particular day or your circumstances, which are always changing and usually not that great. That's pretty much guaranteed in a sin-filled, broken world. But He is always the same. He is unchanging and trustworthy. Every single person in our world will fail us on some level, just like we fail them. But God cannot fail. Our present feelings and "life stuff" do not sway who God is.

Oh, the devil doesn't want you to believe in God and His promises! He plants the seeds of doubt and unbelief. He doesn't want you to know who God really is. When you read the Bible, His word, you *really* get to know who He is. When we believe it, we get rid of the doubt. He transitions our faith to not just be words but to actually become like our skin—a real part of us. By faith, we live, move, think, talk, breathe, and *listen* to His voice. Trust that He will show you the way. He has already written your story. He will guide you. You can rest in Him and be full of peace instead of fear, no matter what comes your way. By faith, we know that we are not in control, and He is. This is freeing and calming. He promises to be with us, one step at a time, one day at a time. I have learned to just "do today" with Him. And when I sense a "loss of control," I have learned to immediately tell Him and ask Him to help. And He does! I had to put verses and His words of truth and promises on my mirror—wherever I could—to remind myself. It became the fabric of my thinking. Constantly seeing His Word gave me an unshakable confidence in a God that loves me and is taking care of me in *everything*. When I started paying attention to everything around me, I found Him in all of it. I call them the God winks.

One by one, all my idols were dethroned. All of these *things* I kept putting my trust in got pulled out from under me. Over and over, my idols continue to be demolished. Literally. I now recognize the evil stuff is Satan and his armies trying to sway our faith. But God turns it to good. It's a massive spiritual battle for our worship.

My Identity—*Who Am I?* vs. *Who I Am*

My core identity went through an enormous change. Before God opened my eyes, I kept looking for "who I am" in all my circumstances, people I was with, my job, my kids, etc., but *not* in Him and who *He* says I am. It finally clicked at the London

Hillsong conference. It was a defining moment in my life. It was a renewal, a deep reviving. My soul was awakened to the Spirit within me. He breathed His breath into me and branded the truth of His presence within me. It was the turning point of my shaky and somewhat shallow faith. The roots suddenly grew deeply rooted in the knowledge of who God is and who He says I am. It was a marker on my journey, flipping my understanding of "what He does" (I had that one down pat from a lifetime of church teaching) to "*who* He is."

Who He is and who I am are directly related. My identity comes from who God says I am. And if He is unchanging and speaks love and truth, my identity cannot change. I will not be shaken. I will not be moved. I am who He says I am.

Psalm 59:16-17 says, "*But as for me, your strength shall be my song of joy. At each and every sunrise, my lyrics of your love will fill the air! For you have been my glory-fortress, a stronghold in my day of distress. O my strength, I sing with joy your praises! O my stronghold, I sing with joy your song! O my Savior, I sing with joy the lyrics of your faithful love for me!*" I *must* "sing with joy the lyrics of His faithful love for me." Even when it *feels* bad, my identity remains steadfast in Him. I know that I am deeply loved, redeemed, and honored by God!

I've heard Louie Giglio say, "The Enemy wants to define you by your scars. Jesus wants to define you by His." Satan wants you and me fixated on the scars of our lives. The *bad* stuff. The sin choices that I have made or the ways others have hurt me. My broken relationships seem to hurt me the most. I could easily define myself by these, but Jesus says, "No, my child, my beautiful, precious daughter! Look at the scars of my hands and feet. Look at what I did for you! These scars from my death on the cross are for you. I died to save you from all of those sins. My scars *heal* you. Forever. My scars call you *mine*." This resolves my personal fear of death. I have an eternal hope of Heaven where there will be no more tears or sorrow or cancer or death.

Overcoming Fear

I lost my fear of aging the month I was diagnosed with metastatic breast cancer. It is amazing what a terminal diagnosis can inspire. This was my Facebook post:

> "It's my 44th birthday. I'm sitting at the social security office today, applying for disability with a Metastatic Breast Cancer diagnosis looming before me. I'm mostly at peace, determined to figure this out, beat this thing inside of me that does not belong. I have so much time to sit and just people watch since it's a government-run office. An hour goes by. I see the cutest old couple arm in arm. I'm not sure who is supporting whom but it doesn't really matter. I imagine at that age

they just support each other, together. I envy the old woman's wrinkles. I want to have wrinkles like that one day. I want to grow old. I'd like to stay in shape but I want lines on my face. Those creases symbolize years of life. Years of life that I want to live. I need this, I think. I WANT to be an old lady. I've never had this thought before. I now long to age. To see my boys go gray. To hear the squeals of their children. To feel the slow and graceful decline of age. Okay, maybe not so graceful. I'll take any or all of it. I'm not quite ready to let my gray hair grow out - don't push it, Han. I like being mistaken for a 20-something year old. I still have a bit of youth and vitality (and vanity, let's face it) on my side. I'm going to embrace it. Stop trying to defy aging, I tell myself. This is a part of life I want to experience like never before. So, Happy Birthday to me. Another year of life to live. Come get me, wrinkles. I'm ready for ya."

The same month I began my hormone blocker treatments, I tattooed the word "fearless" in a very pretty feminine script on my back. Maybe it was a preemptive strike on my very fear-filled heart of what I thought and anticipated would be coming. But it became a declaration on my life. God heard this scared girl's prayer (and undoubtedly that of many others) and He began a transformation in my heart that could only be His doing. It was the beginning of months of heartbreak, and the start of my heart healing in His truth and love. I was beginning to understand what real peace and dependency were. It wasn't in a man. It was in the very Creator of my body and soul. My Redeemer. In my fear, I lost my way and focus. I was caught up in the reality of this world and not of the things of Heaven. Over the next few months He would show me how to do this. On Valentine's Day, just eight weeks after I began treatment, my scans came back clear.

A friend recently asked me, "Is worry a sin?" My answer was, "Yup!" Fear and worry are basically the results of unbelief—not believing He will do what He promises. This is why we need to *know* His promises. We need to keep confessing our unbelief and ask for *great faith*. It's a journey of learning to trust Him implicitly. When we keep letting go of how we think our lives should go, we embrace the future He has planned for our good and His glory! Fear is essentially rooted in pride. It is a result of living in the small world of "Me, Myself, and I." When we live to serve ourselves, we bear the fruits of anger, anxiety, depression, fear, resentment, bitterness, untrustworthiness, arrogance, and addiction. We make ourselves our god.

God invites us into His world. There we find the Triune God: the Father, Jesus the Son, and the Holy Spirit. When we live in the Spirit, filled with Him, we bear His fruit: love, joy, peace, patience, kindness, goodness, faithfulness, gentleness, and self-control (Galatians 5:22-23 NIV). The Spirit works in and through us by His divine nature *in us*. This should make us strong, confident warrior-women, not weak, feeble, or questioning ourselves. Romans 8:6 is worth repeating: *"For the mind-set of the flesh is death, but the mind-set controlled by the Spirit finds life and peace."*

He is slowly peeling back my tightly clenched fingers of control. I'm learning to open my hand and *let* Him. It's not that scary after all! What is actually scary is *me* trying to write my own story! I tried that. I tried to fill the voids of divorce with busy work, with friendships, with food, with pleasure. But none of it really satisfied. *"Consider it a sheer gift, friends, when tests and challenges come at you from all sides. You know that under pressure, your **faith-life** is forced into the open and shows **its true colors**. So don't try to get out of anything prematurely. Let it do its work so that you become mature and well-developed, not deficient in any way"* (James 1:2-4 MSG).

It has not always been this way for me. I have let fear overwhelm me. I have taken matters into my own hands. And I have failed miserably living that way. I live with the pain of my sin choices, which have broken my heart and those of others whom I love. It is true that you usually serve what you fear. I don't want to die having lived a life fearing what others may say or do. I want to die having lived my life for Jesus. *"If you bow low in God's presence, he will eventually exalt you as you leave the timing in his hands. Pour out all your worries and stress upon him and leave them there, for he always tenderly cares for you"* (1 Peter 5:6-7).

XI: KINGDOM PERSPECTIVES

When we suffer, we might ask, "Why is this happening to me?" God showed me my "why" is that now I get to be a witness for God's love and power. I get to reflect Him in the hard stuff. I get to testify of His faithfulness. And He is changing my "why?" to "what?"—What do You want me to learn?

Job 36:15 (NIV) says, "But those who suffer he delivers in their suffering; he speaks to them in their affliction." My friend, Keely, once sympathized, "I know there's a reason for everything but I can't imagine all the feelings you must be feeling! It must be like a roller coaster."

I replied, "The longer I'm on this roller coaster, the more I'm learning to just throw my hands up in surrender to Him. It's blowing my mind how much peace and freedom He invades me with when I just give it all to Him. I'm not having an instant emotional reaction as much. I'm learning to get a Kingdom perspective on it all. It's really cool!"

The Winks of God

The winks of God are *everywhere*. I see them every day now. I see Him in my ever-present financial needs *constantly* being met, in a "chance" conversation resulting in free attorney advice, or when a friend calls me who ends up praying for me and encouraging me with His clear voice from Heaven after just asking Him for help. Things like this happen over and over again. My boys were growing up into adults and making decisions about college and where they would live. I realized the days were quickly fleeting. I wanted to hold onto them while we could nourish our sweet relationships, brother with brother, and sons with mother. "One last year together, Lord," I breathe in prayer. My second oldest received what amounted to a full scholarship for his first year of college. My diagnosis allowed him to live at home for the first year and skip the meal plan, saving us even more money. This was another huge provision and a great blessing to have our tight-knit boy-clique together for one final year.

He provides beyond what I need every day. He keeps moving generous hearts towards me. Another check. A cash gift. A gift card to travel

East to see my family and friends. An opportunity to escape the intense Phoenix heat and reconnect with friends and family. A chance to go camping in the wilds of Oregon. Another bucket list item checked.

These winks of God bring forth praise. And the praise brings forth deeper faith. And the faith lifts my eyes Up and points my life Up in the presence of my sons, my family, my inner circle. It's Him. It's ALL Him.

My Capital "P" Provider

Throughout this journey, I have witnessed God's provision for me and my boys over and over again. This book would not be complete without me recording some of the ways He has been faithful to us, in small details and crazy-big provisions! I found myself renting a house worth way more than I thought I could afford, with a completely paid-for car and car insurance covered for the next six months. How? I sat in awe. I had been waiting on God to provide what felt like another impossibility—an income. I had enough for one third of my expenses each month. I knew He could provide it either through Long Term Disability or by releasing the levy on my ex-husband's last paycheck that was back-owed. In the waiting, I asked Him for *big* things, so I could get to work doing what He was calling me to do. I also knew that if neither scenario happened (especially on *my* timeline) that He still *held me*. I would remind myself to look around: "I mean LOOK, Han! You have a Stage 4 Breast cancer diagnosis that is stable, four ginormous boys who are fed, and you live in a gorgeous home beyond your financial circumstances. God did that. He does BIG things! Don't start doubting Him NOW!".

For the first five months of the year, I had been learning to "lean into" Him. I admit that, in my weakness, I made some pretty sad and desperate choices, but He kept reminding me, "Child, you are mine. Just come closer, and let Me hold you. I've got this situation. I've got your children. I'm your Father and your Husband. Let Me take care of all of this."

I was learning to be still and let Him fight for me. All He had to do was move a person's heart and thoughts in a department that made the final decision, whether I got approved for disability payments or for the paycheck to be released to me. I *knew* that. He holds hearts in His wise and capable hands. In His time. It's been a wonderful lesson to learn and to share. He's given me amazing friends who are hurting right now and let me walk alongside them in love and encouragement. I've now been there. I know how good it can be to walk in the valley and still know peace—an incredible peace that is beyond understanding. It's there, Reader. Grab hold of it. His name is El Ro'i, the God Who Sees me (Genesis 13:16). He knows my need. He is Provider.

The Long Term Disability office made their final decision to deny my claim. I was in a store with my bestie when they called and, I admit it, I cried. As I wiped my tears I prayed, "God help me. You know my end from the beginning. I trust You to provide for me and my boys." You can still be brave and cry. I was learning it is okay to grieve when yucky stuff happens. God built us as emotive beings. I was also learning to not get lost in my grief. In faith, I trusted Him for my finances, too.

Within a week of that decision, I received a letter from the Disability Insurance Company stating that, although they were denying my claim, they were cutting me a check for $2,500 to cover the time I had waited for their decision. Meanwhile, my GoFundMe account still continued to generate unexpected gifts, always at just the right time. I could write all day long about financial gifts given "out of the blue." Someone from my church gifted our family $5,000 the Christmas after my surgery. I stretched those dollars to last the entire year and could even enjoy special treats, birthday gifts, and take out pizza! It's super humbling to be in a position to receive like that. *He* was moving the hearts of people to provide for us. I could easily go to feeling embarrassed or guilty becasuse of it, but someone once told me that the Spirit was behind it, and these generous people were just listening to His prompting. Over and over, through beautiful cousins, family, friends, acquaintances, co-workers, and people I had *never even met*, He provided for me and my boys. He is Yahweh-Yireh, the Lord Will Provide (Genesis 22:14).

Thank you, God, for always being "He Who Provides," especially when I am unfaithful and certainly don't consistently trust You. Thank you for teaching me how to avoid complaining and be thankful that beyond this place is a "Promised Land" of new maturity, blessing, opportunity, and fulfilled promise. Position me to hear what You say or want me to do next.

In July, a child support check held by the bank for 90 days was finally released to me. It was an *abundance* for us, enough to live on for almost five months, and a beautiful, clear message from God to rest in Him. I had to remind myself again: "HE HAS GOT THIS! Why, why, why, do I doubt Him? My weak and feeble faith once again was undergirded with His kind and generous timing. He is a God of abundance! Why do I fear so? I'm once again humbled to my core and simultaneously in AWE of His love and care for me. I lean in. I trust. And I praise."

My friend remarked, "It is amazing to see God taking care of you step by step. Never early and never late."

XII: Use Me, God

God strategically places us at this very point in time to make an impact on our world. Whether it is in our local church, our families, our communities, or on a worldwide stage, He entrusts us to bear our faith shields, like our skin, for the world to see, for the world around us to be encouraged and inspired. I've had people ask me how I could be "so positive" when I have so much loss. They see Him without realizing it. They see His reflection in my life. I read *I'll Have What She's Having* by Bobbie Houston, and it had a profound impact on my life. I realized how much an open, honest display of my life during my hard stuff could impact others around me. The Refiner's Fire I experienced wasn't just for me. My story was going to become a bucket of hope for others. It was there to help douse the flames of others—those still being consumed by the fire—with buckets full of God's Truth and Promises. It is phenomenal to get to do that. He has entrusted me with this purpose. God doesn't waste a thing.

My prayer after my best friend died was this: *hone and shape me, Lord, for a great purpose. Make my pain useful to You.* We get to be God's hands on this earth, a physical representation of His grace in motion. It's our mission in every relationship that we have to make visible the amazing grace of the invisible God.

I am learning how to align myself with His purpose for me. He is teaching me to pause in His presence. Another word for that is *selah.* Sometimes we need a terminal diagnosis to learn that. My scars and wounds tell my story. They aren't pretty, but they are real and true. He overwhelms our failures with His generous grace. My prayer is to be a bold ambassador for Jesus, not living in the fear of man. *Forgive me for when I do live that way. Help me to proclaim You always. Root out the teeny tiny seeds I threw out too haphazardly. Make them flourish anyway.*

I am a warrior-daughter of the King of the world. It's not about my ability but *all* about His. He gives me the ability to overcome fear, to live in His confidence, to do all that is in and on my heart when I commit my ways to Him. How does He want to use me? "Encourage one another daily, as long as it is called 'Today,' that none of you may be hardened by sin's deceitfulness" (Hebrews 3:13 NIV).

Faith Like Skin

This is a learning process. I recognize I am on a journey. I have no idea how long I have left on this earth. In reality, no one knows how long they will live! I just have a clearer *sense* of my humanity and mortality. This sounds morbid. And it feels a bit morbid. But I have a great drive to *DO* while I'm alive and relatively healthy.

As I write this, a friend of my youth is mourning the loss of her 22-year-old son. No one is guaranteed tomorrow or even their next hour. Until I was diagnosed with cancer and especially metastatic, I did not live on a terminal basis. I expected to live till I was 80 or 90 something. I mean, don't you? Now statistics say maybe 5-10 years. That puts me at 50-55. Maybe less. Maybe more. I also know I am not a statistic and refuse to become one. I recognize I have science on my side with new drugs coming on the market constantly. But this reality is a new way of thinking for me, this living in the here and now. I don't live in tomorrows. I have to plan a bit because my sons require that (and I do, too, to get good airline deals to visit family) but I really am learning to live in today. What does my hand have to do *today?* Each day is a gift, and I need to live it well. This turns my days into mini-adventures! Brakes have been put on my life, slowing me down to a conscious way of living. I think more about each meal and each encounter with family and friends. All of a sudden, the *stuff* of life doesn't matter as much, such as furniture and possessions. Don't get me wrong, I still love a cute outfit and a beautiful home—these things reflect my artistic Creator. But I'm not focused on rooting my identity in those things anymore. I guess I am actually learning to be more Spirit-minded. All the Bible verses I grew up memorizing and singing are bearing practical fruit in my life.

These are the days I *thank* God for my diagnosis. I mean, who does that? It's a supernatural change in my heart! It's been a wake-up call to what is really important in life and to learn to live in my calling. It has made me ask the question, "What is my spiritual gift? Am I even using it?" I needed this awakening, this transformation in my heart and soul to realize my purpose. I am learning that my spiritual gift is exhortation. My friend from church, Sally, said, "You realize that this literally means goading, like with a prong!" My first reaction was, "No way! I don't want to poke people's hearts!" That feels like a big task for me. But then I see that He has *already* been using me that way. I see it in my own family, in my sons, in broken relationships all around me. My job is to point people Up. I keep telling them that Jesus is the answer—the only true answer to all of our problems. That's sometimes a scary job to have. But now I am living in this new Identity. I am living in the Spirit. I am learning to be His vessel. I get to be His hands, His arms, His feet, His voice—when I use His words, whether to convict or to encourage. What a task! I don't want people to dislike me or get mad at me or stop talking to me. I'm a peacemaker by nature; I always have been. I want everyone to get along! But life is broken all around me. The days that I feel this heavy burden and weight, I take it all to Jesus. And I go to the Psalms and to His promises.

I am learning to take a step back, to get a better and bigger perspective beyond my present circumstances. All the refining I have experienced in the past three years is part of God's divine plan for me. He is molding me. He is teaching me to lean into Him. He is giving me a depth I did not have in my character and spirit. He is giving me substance and a purpose. I recognize this warrior confidence in myself that isn't "me" but *Him in me*. I am learning to hear His whispered call. *"I know that You delight to set your truth deep in my spirit. So come into the hidden places of my heart and teach me wisdom"* (Psalm 51:6).

I want to live and work for Him. I am asking Him to show me what that means and how that looks. I want to be faithful, not fearful. I want to live with my faith looking like visible skin so that when you see me, you see Him. When you know me, you know Him. What a tall order! What a humbling place to be. *Use me, Jesus. Help me reflect You even in all of my imperfections. Like Bobbie Houston says in her book, let people see me and say, "I'll have what she's having."*

Epilogue

You didn't know this was a love story, did you? When I first started writing this book, I thought it was a story about meeting the love of my life and it turned into meeting the Hope of Heaven. God became my First Love. I cried a lot and felt a lot of loss learning the lessons that I needed to in order that I would learn that God was orchestrating every single step of my life.

I have learned that I am empowered by the Holy Spirit and can live my life unafraid and let my light of faith shine to everyone around me—even when people fail me or betray me, or my body is growing cancer, or I experience the tragedy of the death of my very best friend. My life cannot be bleak because I have the very greatest Hope of Heaven with me. He forgives me. He restores me. He holds me. He carries me. He helps me. He heals me.

Despite all of the losses, I see Him restoring what the locusts have eaten. He is giving me a hope and a dream for my future that's secure in Him and full of love and joy. The loss in this world could be too great to bear except for His great love that awoke my soul and filled the holes. He broke down my walls. He rescued me when He could have left me. He gave me a new song. He whispered His truth into my ear and spoke loudly, "Tell them. Testify. I have done it for you and I will do it again. Over and over I AM. I AM present. I AM love. I AM yours. I fill up what the enemy destroys. I mend what he breaks. I am victorious. Always the Victor. Always Holy. Always Just. Even when it doesn't look like it or feel like it. I AM. I always keep My Promises. Forever Sure. Forever Amen."

So after I wrote the content of this book, I DID meet the love of my life. And I married him.

Visit
www.livinghopecancerfoundation.com
to contact Hannah, book her to speak, and find help for:

— Lifestyle

— Nutrition

— Online support groups

— Prayer

or email her at
hannah@livinghopecancerfoundation.com

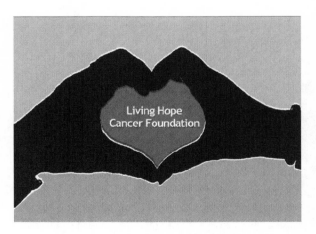